AF176525

TRAVELGUIDE

Mykonos

2021

**ADVERTISING AND SPONSOR FREE
FOR THE RECOMMENDATIONS WERE NO
FREE SERVICES TAKEN**

Information as of Dec. 2020

Published by Apostolos Nikolaidis

FSC
www.fsc.org
MIX
Papier aus ver-
antwortungsvollen
Quellen
Paper from
responsible sources
FSC® C105338

imprint

Picture credits page 76
© 2020 Apostolos Nikolaidis
Production and Publishing: BoD - Books on
Demand, Norderstedt.
ISBN 9783752643930

Two groups of tourists are definitely wrong on Mykonos: the friends of classic sightseeing (there is not enough to see for that - except Delos) and guests who want to rest.

On the other hand, those who love parties, hustle and bustle and shopping are in the right place. Friends of contemporary art also love Mykonos because of its numerous galleries. And nowhere (except perhaps Santorini) does one have such a fantastic view of the Aegean Sea with its almost unreal sunsets. Mykonos was and still is considered very liberal, which is why it is a popular destination for gays and lesbians, but without being intrusive. Loose, casual and tolerant: that is Mykonos.

Mykonos is also known as the "Island of the Wind" and rightly so. During the "hot" months of July to September, the north wind, the Meltemi, ensures much lower temperatures than in Germany. It is therefore often only really hot in the low season of May and October.

(Hottest day in 2020 was October 5 (!) with 33 degrees) The wind can be extremely disturbing and cool. Therefore, you always need a jacket for cooler wind evenings - even in July/August! And if you ask yourself, "Why did I pack long-sleeved shirts in this heat?": It's guaranteed to blow in gusts of cold wind the next day.

And we are not talking about Southern German wind (bft 1-2), but about 4-6 bft normal with unpleasant gusts up to 8 bft.

You hate wind? You love wearing hats? Then you better cancel your trip.

Arrival

The airport is a small island airport, operated by Fraport and gradually rebuilt. The modern arrival terminal is already completed. mostly you walk from the plane to the terminal.

The airport is right on the edge of Mykonos Town (max 10 minutes from the center, in Greek "Chora"). Even to the other end of the island (Kalafati) the transfer time is not more than 25 minutes.

Flights from the UK are offered by BA and easyjet, but they are rare. **For connection flights Munich/Frankfurt and Vienna are the best hubs.**

Do not use Athens as hub, as the 20-Minutes flight to Mykonos is mostly more expensive than the flight to Athens.

 Mykonos is currently connected to Central Europe directly by Condor, Air Baltic, Aegean, Eurowings, Easyjet, Ryanair, **from Germany,** Ryanair and Wizz **from Vienna,** Edelweiß from **Zurich** and XXX from **Paris**.   Unfortunately, the flights only start at the beginning of May and end around the 18th of October, although the weather can still be summery well into November.

Current information including flight plan for 2021 can be found on page 68!

Watch the differences in the calendar (Greece is orthodox). For 2021: Easter and Whitsun are FOUR weeks later than in the West.

Information about entry to Greece and Corona: page 79.

Taxi transfer to the center costs between 12-14 €.

Taxis are generally cheaper than in Central Europe, but most of the time you wait a long time until a taxi arrives (taxi rank: promenade - next to the monument).

There are 3 ports on Mykonos, the name of which can be misleading.
The OLD HARBOR is the historic on the waterfront.

Later, at the other end of the promenade, a new harbor was built, but today it is usually called OLD PORT. From there, only the trips to Delos or the SEABUS to the NEW PORT start.

Buy your tickets at the office on the waterfront promenade. There are usually no queues.

 The big ferries arrive at the **NEW PORT,** located 1 km north of the old town. There is a bus shuttle from Old Port. DO NOT walk to the NEW PORT, because there is NO sidewalk.

The following ports are connected:
Piraeus (Athens), Rafina (Athens), Heraklion (Crete), Santorin,
Ios, Naxos, Paros, Kiathos, Syros, Thessaloniki and Tinos.
From the NEW PORT (every 30 Min. between 7.30 am and 11.30 pm) the SEABUS-Boat goes to the

historic harbor on the promenade (journey time 5 min, 2 Euro). Since there are enough parking spaces in the harbor in the evening, it is a comfortable and nerve-sparing alternative to car trips to the old town, especially for tourists who stay outside Mykonos Town.
www.mykonos-seabus.gr

General Data

Mykonos belongs to the Cyclades in the Aegean Sea. The island is just under 100 square kilometers large with about 15,000 inhabitants. In length Mykonos measures about 25 km.

There are only two settlements in our sense: Mykonos Town (Chora) and the small village of Ano Mera. Delos is a separate island, but the origin of the settlement. (see DELOS). A third uninhabited island is Renia.

The name Cyclades refers to the Greek "kyklos" = ring, so Mykonos is one of the "Ring islands"!

Town Centre with Old Town

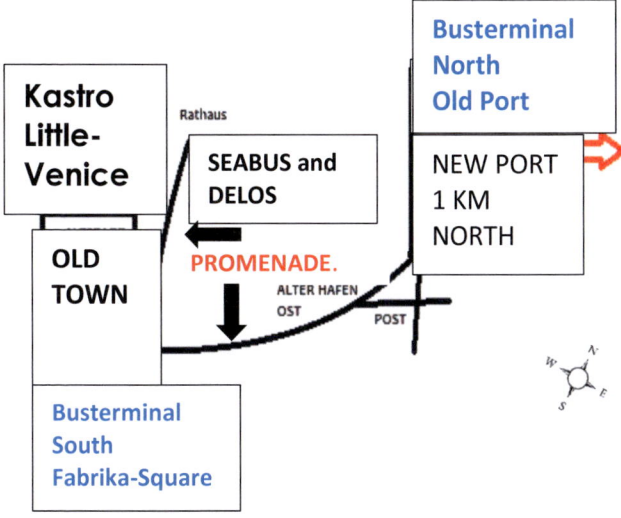

Again – and important in summer for getting to the town centre: From the NEW PORT (cruise) every hour between 7.30 am and 11.30 pm SEABUS-boat goes to the historic harbor on the promenade (journey time 5 min, 2 Euro). Since there are enough parking spaces in the harbor in the evening, it is a comfortable and nerve-sparing alternative to car trips to the old town, especially for tourists who stay outside Mykonos Town.
www.mykonos-seabus.gr

Driving on Mykonos is considered dangerous, but not only because of the Greek driving style. Rather, the roads are in poor condition, very narrow and full of potholes.

Scheme Traffic Mykonos

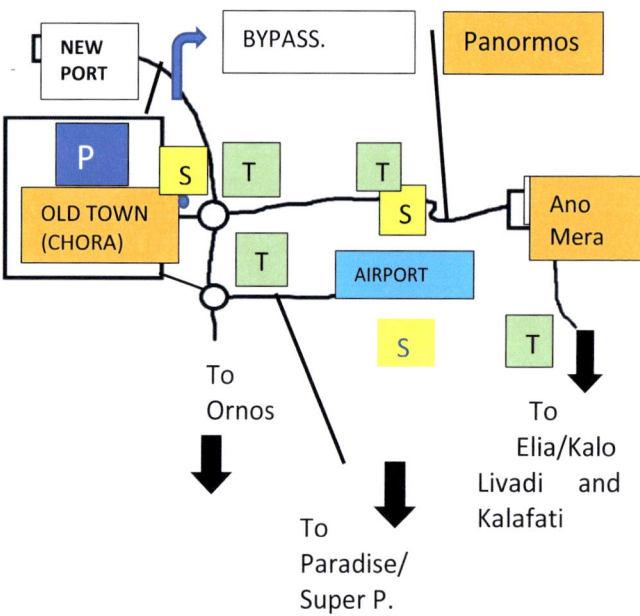

S **SUPERMARKET**
T **Gas Station**

Detailled map island page 40 / old town page 77.
Add to that hundreds of ATVs (or quads) that are driven by tourists, who have never driven an ATV before. It is the tourists who make driving so

dangerous. Faster than 50 km / h in the peak-time? Forget it. Be happy if you don´t be in one of the normal traffic jams.

Police is not on the road and leaves tourists mostly alone. When returning to the car always check if your car has been hit. Accident escape is often considered a minor offense among younger tourists (and they are not always sober). The police plays no role in Mykonos with their 8 men per shift. The helmet duty exists, but no one controls it.

Always pay attention to oncoming traffic. Greeks overtake in traffic and ignore solid lines.

A big problem is the parking in the center or on some beaches (see beaches + P-card.)

AT THE NORTH END OF THE OLD TOWN (DIRECTION NEW HARBOR) YOU WILL FIND A LARGE PARKING PLACE (to be paid est. in 2020 - so far free)
If you want to go to Mykonos Town, follow the signs **"CHORA"!**

Car-/Quad-Rental

On Mykonos you need a vehicle, because almost all beaches are outside the city, especially the beautiful ones. Although there is a public bus system, standing in a crowded bus at 30 degrees for 20 minutes is not for everyone.

Attention: When refueling you have to wait for the gas station attendant, self-service is not allowed. With unleaded 95 you are usually right. Fuel is generally extremely expensive in Greece, plus the island surcharge. Gas stations can be found on all main roads (direction and in Ano Mera, direction Ornos and direction New Harbor).

The prices for rental cars offered by the big companies are even with advance booking partly grotesque high, the vehicles mostly damaged (so take photos when you take the car). Book your car / ATV / motorcycle on site.
Note:
Quads are a good choice given the lack of parking space**. But: you should not skimp on performance,** otherwise you do not get up the hills from the beach, especially if you are two! A big mistake!

Again: Take photos of damages!

Car Rental Sahas, Mykonos-Tagoo (Nord)
Tel: +30 22890 22112
Mobile +30 693 6826864
rentals@sahas-mykonos.gr

Above the shore road towards New Port. Inexpensive, impeccable vehicles and good service - this is what sets this car rental company apart. They pick you up from the airport/port and bring you back to the airport for free at the end of the holiday. Alternatively, you can leave it at your hotel. They are always friendly and helpful.

The car rental also includes apartments and suites that are reasonably priced and very well equipped (see "Overnight accommodation / Apartments"

Supermarkets

Before the actual "shopping" still some hints for self-catering. Until recently, there were no large supermarkets in Greece, because they wanted to protect the countless mom and pop shops (mini-markets). On Mykonos there are now three large supermarkets: one at the ring road from the port to the roundabout ("AB") and from the roundabout towards Ano Mera, after 300 meters on the right ("proton"). The third one is near the airport **– with own DJ**. Most goods are expensive, but that's more because especially food is very cheap at home. All supermarkets are open until 9 pm, Sundays only in the mornings. On Sundays you can go to the numerous mini markets.

ATMs

ATMs are more than 30 spread over the island, some directly on the beaches (Ornos and Kalafati). They are provided with the international symbol ATM. The ATMs of Piraeus Bank and Alpha work without any problems - the others sometimes squat (Euronext).

In the old town there are countless places (for example at the Alphabank and between taxi rank and harbor). As a rule, you do not go to the bank, because opening hours are curious according to our standards.

Shopping

For shopping in Mykonos: there is everything your heart desires, but at high prices. The special feature is the large number of small boutiques and shops that offer the exquisite and extraordinary and soothe the offer of the usual chain stores.
There are no shopping malls on Mykonos. The whole old town is THE shopping mall.
Especially the galleries of Mykonos enjoy international reputation. With the appropriate purse the spectacular sculpture or the innovative painting is yours.
As in the whole of Greece, linen goods (shirts and blouses) are typical and usually cheaper than in the rest of Europe. Beware of "discount badges" especially in chain stores: pay attention to the original price. There are from mid-September discounts on clothing and shoes. Clearance sales begin in the first days of October. More about shopping and the galleries later under "Old Town".

Cigarettes currently cost 4,10 euros per packet. Kiosks with a large selection (including cigars) can be found at the roundabout direction to Ano Mera and in the center next to the taxi stand at the eastern end of the waterfront. By the way: Allowed are – within the EU - 800 cigarettes. You can also buy the rods in Duty-Free on the return flight.

Security

In general, small islands - due to lack of escape routes - are particularly safe. This also applies to Mykonos. However, thefts from open cars are increasing. For Gays / Lesbians, Mykonos is one of the safest places ever. There have been no incidents in recent years. No wonder: the danger for the attacker would be far too great, 30 % of the guests are gay.

BEACHES

First of all, the Aegean is not a warm sea. Due to the cool north wind ("Meltemi", the water is by no means a bathtub. Even in midsummer months, the water temperature is at max. 24 degrees - welcomed in the heat of course, in the low season, it is usually too cool (October about 20 degrees).
The beaches in the Aegean are no Caribbean beaches. They are mostly small sandy beaches, often framed by rocks. Our beach recommend- dations are based on beauty, which means: what we consider a beautiful beach - sand, width, beautiful location and if possible also dunes ... The

famous party beaches Paradise and Super Paradise follow at the end, because here beauty plays no role. Who goes there wants only two things: party and sex.

Public buses run to almost all beaches.
These are often overcrowded and transfer times partly long (Kalafati). The central bus terminal is located at Fabrika Square.

The Fabrika Square is located at the southern end of the old town (waterfront promenade = northern end, see plan page 7 and 77.)
At the OLD PORT there is another (to the New Port and Agios Stefanos).

The fare depends on the destination but is usually less than 2 euros. Night buses are a bit more expensive.

Alternatively, there is the possibility of beach-hopping by boat - getting out where you like it. No stress with driving, parking or bus. In the low season but not all beaches are approached. Sometimes the tours start only at Platos Gialos. Please inquire currently in the hotel or at the counter.

1 PANORMOS / PARKING NO PROBLEM

Panormos is considered the most beautiful beach of Mykonos. It is wide and long, the only one with dunes, with a fantastic view of the bay, where often sailing ships are on site.

The beach is about 15 minutes from the center and the only big north beach. Here it is often a few degrees cooler than the other beaches in the south of the island due to the north wind (therefore you should always have a large bath towel for wrapping). Spectacular is the descent down to the beach: a magnificent view of the sea and the beach.

The beach is run by the Club Principote - www.principote.com - a club complex with bars, restaurants and beach service. Access for everyone possible, but a bit expensive. About a cappuccino for 8 euros or a pizza for 40 euros you should not be surprised. For the atmosphere is maintained during the day, the sanitary facilities exclusive. Of course, you can also lay down in the dunes for free.

On-site parking in large numbers.

Up the hill there are some smaller and cheaper restaurants.

If you are good on foot, you can reach the small beach located in the north on steep steps, in the off-season you are sometimes completely alone. A little further north is AGIOS SOSTIS, a very beautiful beach that mainly islanders visit. The restaurant "Kikis" is a perennial favorite, even among Greeks.

.

2 KALO LIVADI (SOLYMAR) PARKING NO PROBLEM

There are also "secret tips" in terms of beaches on Mykonos. Kalo Livadi is still spared from the masses. A beautiful, fine sandy beach, 15 minutes from the center in the southeast. Access via / via Ano Mera, behind the petrol station to the left before descending left to Kalafati, go straight ahead and then down to Kalo Livadi. The beach area has just been renovated, the road is laid behind the restaurants and the old street is planted. The Solymar is an excellent restaurant, also the beach service nimble and friendly. But not cheap, because: Kalo Livadi is considered a celebrity beach. All around are the most expensive villas. (hence the brisk helicopter traffic). Since celebrities often avoid the hustle and bustle, they go to Kalo Livadi rather than to the Paradise beaches. Kalo Livadi is not marked on many cards to keep the "infantry" out. There is no bus to this beach.

3 KALAFATI PARKING NO PROBLEM

Kalafati is located in the southeast of the island, 20 minutes from the center (30 minutes by bus). Follow the signs to Ano Mera, through the town and then always following the main road. Again, there is a spectacular view of the sea and the beach. The beach is the longest on Mykonos and a pure sandbeach. Because of the wind

conditions, it is THE windsurfing beach. Windsurfing shop right on the beach (www.pezi-huber.com), with the possibility of taking lessons.
At the upper end there is an inexpensive restaurant with panoramic windows on the left. Below are loungers and sun chairs, which are free of charge.
At the far end you will find the "Aphrodite", rather exclusive and expensive, built into the sea.

4 ORNOS PARKING NO PROBLEM

Ornos is a quiet, sheltered beach, also for families, as the sea is shallow.
Coming from the center (no matter if on the bank- or bypass road) you reach the **Inner Bay** with a free parking lot (next are 2 bakeries and a supermarket). The Inner beach is reserved for kite surfers – it is too windy for normal tourists.
From there it is still 300 m to the **Outer beach**, called "**Ornos Beach"** ATTENTION: Follow the sign "Ornos Beach". Right next to it is a road that only supposedly leads to the beach!
On the beach there are two good restaurants and a nice bar, with mostly Greek guests (behind the ATM). Going to the left, you will come across a very good restaurant, the "Apaggio" - with moderate prices for this location.
.

Ornos Kite-Surfer-Strand

5 ELIA PARKING NO PROBLEM

Granted: Elia is not easy to reach: first to and through Ano Mera, behind the gas station RIGHT (on the left it goes to Kalafati) and then it goes down on tight serpentines. But then expect a wide sandy beach. Right on the beach is a good restaurant with reasonable prices. In recent years, Elia developed as the main gay beach (right of the rainbow flag), especially for older gays (means older than 25 😊).

Above is one of the island's best hotels, the
Myconian Imperial Resort & Thalasso Spa Center.

Elia

6 FTELIA PARKING NO PROBLEM

At the southern end of the north bay lies Ftelia, a beach popular among windsurfers, just to the left of the main road to Ano Mera. Exit left to the S-curves. Granted: the driveway looks like the moon landscape. At the end of the road turn right. Behind the big rock lies one of the most beautiful small bays of the island, including a good restaurant / beach club ("Alemagou"), which was built into the hill - www.alemagou.com

7 AGIOS STEFANOS PARKING DIFFICULT

Agios Stefanos is the city closest beach, about 1 km north of the city, above the NEW PORT. Who is not lazy, takes the sea-bus from the old to the new harbor, from there it is still 500 m on foot, but rising. From the Old Port but also drives a bus to Ag. Stefanos.
It is one of the quieter beaches, with an excellent restaurant 50 meters above the beach, the "Limnios" There are also many Greeks, always a good sign.

8 Paradise/Super Paradise PARKING DIFFICULT

Why are the best-known beaches landing at the end of the ranking list? Precisely for this reason. If you expect beauty and tranquility from a beach, you are in the wrong place.

For those who want house music and bustle from noon on, Paradise is truly a paradise. Especially at night, when the Tropicana and Cavo Paradiso clubs are THE night locations of the island.

Paradise was originally a pure gay beach. As more and more heterosexuals spread there, gays and lesbians moved one bay eastwards to Super Paradise.

The taxi to Paradise / Super Paradise costs about 15 €.

Super Paradise

9 Paraga PARKING DIFFICULT

A bay off Paradise (to the west) is Paraga, a small sandy beach less crowded than the Paradise beaches.
At Paraga you will find the "Scorpios" the currently hottest beach club.

Paraga

10 Platis Gialos PARKING A NIGHTMARE

A beach to forget. Completely built up. The sunchairs stand partially in the water and so tight that you can easily enjoy the body odor of the neighbors. Please: There are so many beautiful beaches, you certainly do not have to come here. In addition, parking is a nightmare. The road just ends - and then you are helpless.

11 A SECRET TIP: FOKO

A beach for you alone? On some days this only possible in Foko, in the northeast of the island. No clubs, just one (good) restaurant: beach, clean and peace. Difficult the directions: In Ano Mera **the first left**, then another 15 minutes through the "Little Canyon" of Mykonos.

Foko

Beach in the southwest, small and with little parking space. Above are the really expensive resorts, but to which one has no access. Access via Ornos.

Worth knowing

Valet parking
Is widely common on Mykonos. Because of the lack of parking space, you are not allowed to park in some places, but this is done by the parking attendant to park the cars tighter. When picking usually a tip of 2 Euro is enough.

Public holidays
Are important because Mykonos is Greek Orthodox, means: In normal years Easter and Pentecost are a week later than in catholic/protestant countries –
BUT: In 2021 the gap is FOUR WEEKS. Easter is on May 2 - enormously important in the travel planning, because on the Greek Pentecost young Greeks traditionally come to Mykonos and the ticket prices rise dramatically.

Taxis
Are relatively cheap, but rarely found. At the taxi stand on the promenade next to the monument, long lines often form, especially when cruise ships spit out their thousands of tourists. Please check alternatives - the Seabus or the bus.

Opening hours
are much more generous than in Western Europe. Supermarkets open until 21 clock, mini markets even longer. Pharmacies in the city center until 22 o'clock. Even bakeries are open until well into the evening. With the exception of the supermarkets and bakeries you have to prepare for a siesta between 15.00 and 18.00.

Post / Telephone (OTE)
See map page 6.

Police
Next to the airport
See map page 7.

Medical services
It is best to contact your hotel owner or car rental company, as they often speak English better than the emergency call or the hospital staff. A very good clinic (Hygeia) is located at the large

roundabout (2 houses downhill, behind the kiosk). Don´t forget a private health insurance!

Prices

are significantly higher than on other Greek islands.

The cappuccino is on the beaches between 4 and partly 8 euros, the beer between 5 and 12. Cigarettes and medicines are much cheaper than in most countries. Antibiotics are available without prescription (4 Euro, Amoxicillin 500), like many other medications too).

Internet

Usually fast and also in almost all cafés and restaurants WLAN is available, in most hotels as well. With stick 1 GB currently costs 2.90 euros (D1).

Water

Is as scarce on the island as nowhere else in the Mediterranean. Although there is rainfall in winter, it can´t be tied because the island consists almost entirely of rocks. A reservoir was built near Panormos. This was almost empty in May 2020 and this before the season. In Summer, water often comes by tanker and is of inferior quality. To be used for dental cleaning: maybe, NEVER as drinking water.

And when showering please do not let the water run for minutes.

Bakeries

are well stocked for southern climes in terms of bread, and grain breads are sometimes found. On the road to Ano Mera (400 m right side) you will find the bakery Veneti, a feast for the eyes. In addition to numerous types of bread, the grandiose pies and tartlets in particular delight. Too bad that you can´t take them home. Since 2019 there is also a branch on the promenade.
In Ano Mera you will find the bakery Koutsothanasis right behind the place-name sign. Well sorted and much cheaper than in the city. In the Chora you will also find a very good bakery on the left side of the promenade (seen from the sea).

Earthquakes

Few tourists know that the Aegean is one of the regions of Europe where the earth often rumbles. Just a few days ago, Nov 29, 2020, the Aegean was shaken by a quake (6.2): 39 deaths. Mykonos is relatively safe, as there are no big hotel-buildings.
Nevertheless, take the 30 seconds and look for the next emergency-exit.

THE MUST DO´s

1 The beach of Panormos
2 The beach of Kalo Livadi
3 The beach of Kalafati
4 Sunset in Little Venice (Caprice)
5 A trip to Delos
6 Old Town Tour
7 Beach hopping by boat
8 At least one Orthodox church
9 A club night at "Scorpios" or
"Tropicana"

Typical Greek!?

With the usual prejudices of many Europeans that, the Greeks do not work, we must quickly make short work. Most people in Mykonos work from mid-April to mid-October - WITHOUT a day off. In your bakery you will always meet the same people, whether 10 am in the morning or 9 pm, whether Monday or Sunday - and all that in the permanent heat!

Two small episodes may show, however, that some things are handled quite differently in Greece than in the rest of Europe.

The lamp shop of Mykonos

This refers to the New cruise port, which they probably wanted to make *very* nice and that's why they thought: the more, the better. This was especially true for the streetlamps, so they installed 152 in the most beautiful blue. So, the nickname for the port is "lamp shop" and the assumption, beside the Chinese wall one saw also the port of Mykonos from a space station. The curiosity: on the walkway from the port to the city - extremely dangerous, because next to the road - is not ONE lamp.

The six, no, five windmills

No doubt, the windmills in the Kastro district are the landmark of Mykonos.
But wait: In some photos you can see six intact, on another five windmills. In fact, there were six of them when a Caribbean liquor company held a public relations campaign in one of the six mills. The PR succeeded: the whole mill burned down. The next day, postcard salesmen simply crossed out the mill on the subject. Perhaps typical Greek: what to rebuild? We still have five!

Nightlife

When Central Europeans think of "disco" or "club", they think of cellars in industrial parks.
That a club in the south usually has neither walls nor roofs know only experienced party people, for example. from Ibiza.

The nightlife on Mykonos offers two options: either visit one of the large beach clubs - of course right on the beach - or you make party in the city center. The combination is difficult, because you have to drive to the clubs and taxis are often difficult to get. It's best to call the bartender for a taxi, because he knows a taxi driver, who knows another taxi driver ... you know. Some beach clubs offer night buses
(Cavo Paradiso, Tropicana, Scorpio´s).

For the nightlife in the city applies: the bars are easy to find. Throughout Castro and Little Venice, you will find bars and small clubs that you can already hear from the exaggerated volume at a great distance.

Classics are the "Scandinavian Bar", which is an institution and also has a dance area, and the "Studio 54" near the taxi stand next to the monument.

At the end of the main road Matogianni to the left, you will soon reach the "Bonbonniere", which has a very nice lounge atmosphere before the party starts.

Opposite is the noble bar "Queen of Mykonos" for the rich and sometimes beautiful.

Three bars / dance clubs can be found (practically wise) in the main street Matogianni, which is easy to find (see old town plan):

The Anchor Bar, Bar Uno and Icarus.

Next to the Old Port East is the Yacht Club (open 24 hours).

Of the beach clubs, the following are currently the most popular:

Scorpio´s (Paraga)
Tropicana (Paradise)
Cavo Paradiso (Paradise)
Alemagou (Ftelia)
Principote (Panormos)

But beware! All are extremely expensive and therefore: look at the menu before.
During the season there are always live gigs of hip DJs. Current data can always be found on the facebook/instagram pages of the clubs, the websites are usually not up to date.

For all bars and clubs: Gays / Lesbians are welcome. No wonder - they are mostly in the majority. There are special gay bars (mostly in Kastro) - but like-minded people can be found everywhere.

Faros
Armenistis

Panormos

372 m

1

6

7

Agios
Stefanos

Ftelia

Mykonos
Chora

Ano Mera

275 m

Agios Ioannis
Diakoftis

5

Ornos

Psarroy

Platys
Gyalos

Elia

4

8

9

Paradise/Super
Paradise

Paraga

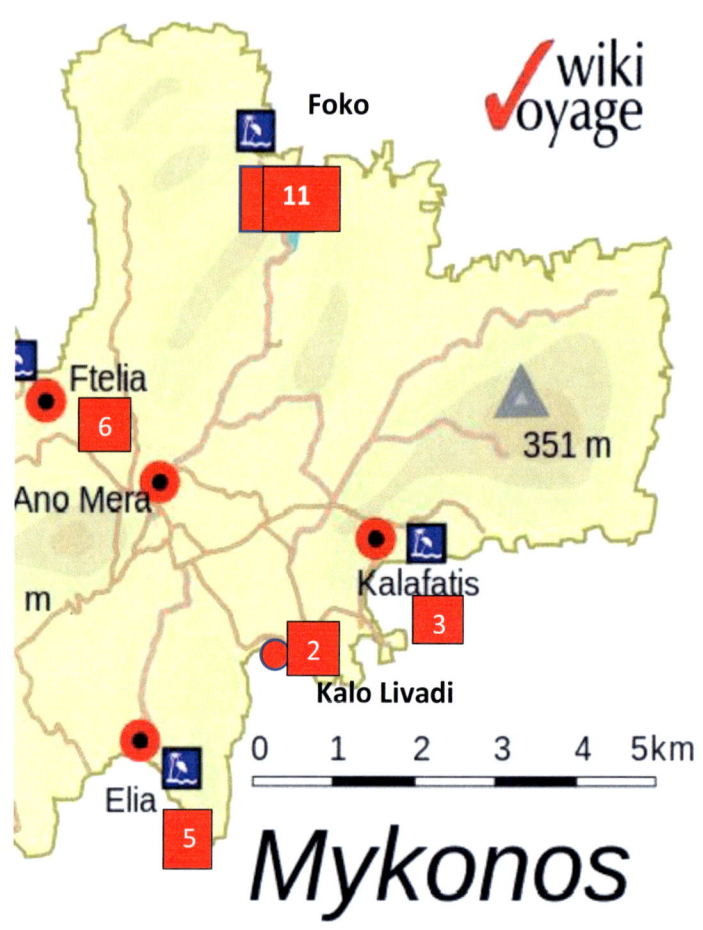

Foko

wiki
oyage

11

Ftelia

6

Ano Mera

351 m

m

Kalafatis

3

2

Kalo Livadi

Elia

5

0   1   2   3   4   5km

Mykonos

Oh dear, this language!

Of course, it is always helpful if you have at least basic knowledge of the language as a tourist. Above all, it's one thing: polite!
But unfortunately, Greek has a high hurdle. They use other letters. Some traffic signs could not be read if they were not bilingual.
That Άνω Μεράς means Ano Mera, you can only guess.

But with a few words you get a friendly smile:

Thanks = efcharisto.
Please = parakalo.
Emphasis on the last syllable.

Welcome and farewell are united in one word: **Jassas!**
Te kanis? = how are you?
Tha ithela ena cappuchino = I would like to have a ... (th as in English).
The formal Kalimera as well as Kalispera and Kalinichta (good day, good evening and good night) are more formal.

There is a small trap with yes and no, because 'yes' in Greek is 'Ne'. Origin of many

misunderstandings. 'No', however, is called Ochi (as in the German "Ich").
You want to curse while driving? No problem: You are an idiot = Ise ilithios, Vlakka = stronger than idiot 😊
Where is …? = Pu ine?
With basic knowledge of English, you get along everywhere. Without English, nothing works!

Did you know...

that the Greek flag is of German origin? The first Greek king after independence was Otto of Bavaria. And he took the Bavarian white-blue colours (not the other way around) to Athens.

THE OLD TOWN

Those who stand on the hill at sunset and look
down on the white-and-blue old town can
understand why Brigitte Bardot said that this is
the most enchanting city in the world. At the
end of the fifties many VIPs were bored of
Nice and St. Tropez and looked for a new
destination. The international jet set (with
Alain Delon, Gunther Sachs, Jackie Kennedy
or Richard Burton and Elisabeth Taylor) went
to Mykonos. As some of the VIPs were gay,
Mykonos became the paradise for gay
people. (That´s why the beach is called
'Paradise'). Today Mykonos is still the

favourite spot for the 'rich and beautiful' but: today they choose protected resorts with their own helicopter space. One isolates himself from ordinary people. Nevertheless, you can still see Leonardo di Caprio or Ben Affleck in the old town, hidden behind a hat and big sunglasses.

The old town is characterized by narrowness and is a single maze, as I am still running today. In that sense, a plan is completely useless. Your tour ends at the promenade? Be lucky! Your round trip leads you to a bus terminal? Then you have arrived at the southern end (Fabrika-Square). The advantage of the Labyrinth: You keep coming to new quarters of the city you've never seen before.

We start our round-trip of the old town on the boardwalk (promenade).

Route 1

Go to the left end of the promenade. You pass the town hall and a small chapel, Agios Nikolaos. If it does not go any further, go up the stairs.

Now you are in the districts KASTRO and LITTLE VENICE. The first name goes back to the ancient fortress, built in the 13th century by the Venetians, but of which little has remained.

In Kastro is also one of the most famous churches in Greece, the Panagia Paraportiani. The name ("next to the gate") indicates that there was the entrance to the old castle. There are five interconnected chapels, four of them on the ground floor. The building dates are difficult to determine, probably the first chapel dates from the 14th century.

The name Little Venice is a bit exaggerated and there are no channels through the district, but the rows of houses facing the sea stand on posts and protrude into the sea (see picture next page). This was the easiest way for merchants to load the ships. Sit down in one of the cocktail bars (best: the "Caprice") and enjoy the sunset. With the grandiose silhouette of Little Venice a great picture. Unfortunately, more and more Chinese, who often obstruct the view, conquer the place. When the obligatory photo is taken, they are mostly gone. The cocktail bars of the district are the meeting points of the VIPs, where € 30,000 for a bottle of champagne are quite common. But do not worry: there are also drinks for the normal purse (cocktails from 12 €).

Above the cocktail bars stands the landmark of Mykonos: the (now) five windmills. There is nothing special about the mills, they served the same purpose as everywhere else in the world: the flour milling. In the past, the whole island was littered with windmills. There are only a few copies left.

The "mascot" of Mykonos is the pelican. A "copy" of the original from 1958 mostly walks through the windmill area. But there is no historical background. Below the windmills is a small beach, next to the Panagia Theotokos Pigadiotissa, the richly decorated bishop's church of the city. A stone's throw away is the only Roman Catholic church on the island.

Route 2

starts again on the waterfront. At the other end of the promenade stands the monument to Manto Mavrogenous, a female freedom fighter who succeeded in foiling the landing of Turkish troops in the Greek War of Independence in 1822.

On the old town side begins the main street, the Matogianni.

Church in Matogianni (Agia Kiriaki)

Not a wide shopping boulevard, but a lane two meters wide. Stressful tightness is so preprogrammed in midsummer.

Passing expensive boutiques and countless galleries you will reach on the right-hand side the Museum of Local History ("House of Lena") and the Maritime Museum. The best way is to follow the crowd to the right, as this will bring

you back to the promenade and not be lost.
Because of the countless streets with
confusing names and no signs, a rough
outline will help you the most.

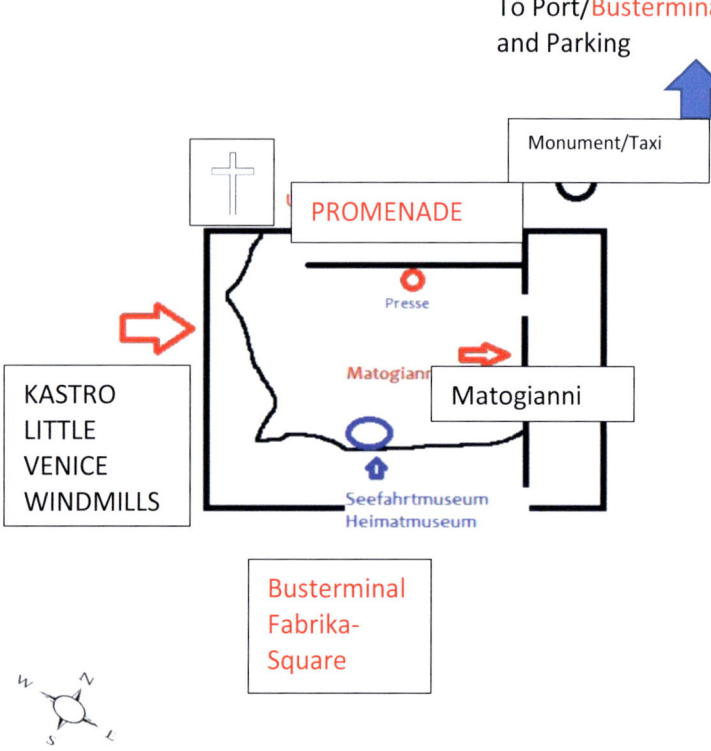

To Port/Bustermina and Parking

Monument/Taxi

PROMENADE

Presse

KASTRO
LITTLE
VENICE
WINDMILLS

Matogianni

Matogianni

Seefahrtmuseum
Heimatmuseum

Busterminal
Fabrika-
Square

A map can be found on page 77, but because of the missing signs, it helps only little. But since even experienced Mykonos guests get lost regularly, let yourself drift!
You will always find yourself in new streets!

Ano Mera

Next to Mykonos Town, Ano Mera is the only other significant settlement with village character. Since the island is very small, almost the entire area is built, a spatial separation between settlement and nature as ours does not exist. And of course, the wealthy residents like to have a little distance to neighbors.

Ano Mera is located right in the center of the island.

Right at the entrance to the village is a superb bakery (Koutsothanasis). Semi-right runs the old main street, mostly parked.

Stay on the new main road and turn right after 200 m, up the hill. There is a large parking lot with cash machine and a large supermarket (flora).

You are just behind the market square of Ano Mera, surrounded by numerous restaurants, all with down-to-earth cuisine and a bit cheaper than in the city.

Right next to the market square is the largest (or only) church in Mykonos, because all other church houses are strictly "just" chapels. The church belongs to the monastery of Panagia Tourliani and can be visited daily from 9-13 and 18-21 h. Founded in 1542, it was plundered by pirates in the 16th century.

Mykonos has many nicknames, "Island of the Wind", "Party Island" or "Celebrity Island". Equally correct would be "Island of the Chapels".

More than 100 small churches can be found scattered around the island, often in completely surprising or lonely places.

Anyone moaning at the word "church visit" should remember one thing: Perhaps it is your first contact with the Orthodox Church, which in many ways differs from the Catholic/ Protestant counterpart.

Visible with every glance in an orthodox chapel: lovingly, partly splendidly decorated, with big crystal chandeliers and icons, they are "more "cosy" than our places of worship. About 80% of the inhabitants of Mykonos are orthodox.

Also keep in mind that the church calendar is different. Easter and Pentecost are a week later than ours, 2021 four weeks

In general, the island was always the target of pirates. The strong north wind made the landing difficult, but there were no permanent troops on Mykonos. Neither Venetians nor Ottomans considered this as necessary.

Monastery in Ano Mera

Ϝistory of Mykonos

 Mykonos itself is historically little significant.
Rather, it is the nearby island of Delos,
historically of great relevance to all of
Greece.

Delos was for centuries the most important city in the entire Aegean with at times over 25,000 inhabitants. Unimaginable, you can see today the small, uninhabited island (more details under "Delos").

So today's Mykonos town was initially only a kind of suburb of Delos, on which was probably one of the cemeteries of Delos, because graves were banned on Delos due to the lack of space.

1500 BC

Delos is developing into a city of supraregional importance.

700-393 BC

Delos becomes the political and religious center of the Aegean and is temporarily meaning Athens. The city grows to 25,000 inhabitants.

166 BC

The Romans are the new rulers.

395 -1204

for nearly 1000 years Mykonos comes under Byzantine administration.

1207 - 1390
The Republic of Venice conquers the island.
Mykonos becomes a trading post.

1537
For the first time Mykonos becomes Muslim -
the Ottomans are there and remain until
1822, mostly represented only by
administrative officials.

1822
Under Mavro Mavrogenous Mykonos defends
itself against an Ottoman invasion -
successfully. Mykonos becomes Greek.

1940
 Mykonos comes under Italian administration.
German soldiers were never on Mykonos.
Mykonos was too unimportant. Naxos,
however, was German.

Since 1930
Beginning of tourism with 3,000 guests per
year.

1960
As the hustle and bustle of the Nice, St. Tropez
and Cannes jet sets has become increasingly
crowded, celebrities were seeking for a new,

untouched destination and discovered Mykonos.

1981
Mykonos becomes part of the EU.
As a result, the infrastructure has been massively improved - the bypass-road and the New Port were built.

Monument to Mavro Mavrogenous.

Delos

Mykonos without Delos is like Rome without Coliseum. Even art buffs should overcome themselves - it's worth it.

You can choose between two options: a pure transfer with exploration of the island on your own. The museum on the island gives you the necessary overview.

Of course, you can also book a combination of boat trip and guided tour, currently daily in English (see following pages).

Note: On Delos there is virtually no shade, sun protection and water recommended.

Delos

In ancient times the small Delos played a major role in the Aegean. Two reasons: First, because of its location in the middle of the Aegean Sea. Around Delos, the other islands of the Cyclades are grouped as in a' Kyklos' (ring), and it is also roughly in the center between Athens, Crete and Asia Minor. On the other hand, the island was a religious centre.

Two Greek gods were born on Delos: the twins Apollon and Artemis.

Directly behind the harbor begins the archaeological zone with the temple district. Numerous marble pinnacles indicate the base areas of the individual buildings. For the orientation of the visitors serve modern stone tablets with the respective designation of the temple.

The statues, columns and mosaics and the stadium show that Delos was not just a big city, but also the religious center of Greece.

The former pond is marked by a small tamarisk forest, in the middle of which a tall palm tree grows - in memory of the palm, in which Leto gave birth to their children Apollo and Artemis.

The museum is housed in a plain building behind the temple district. It shows statues, mosaics, murals and ceramics from the excavation area. Further south, there is a large area with well-restored remains of antique homes. Sometimes there are mosaics to be found. According to the sculptures or mosaics found, the excavators named the houses: House of the Dolphins, House of the Masks, House of Cleopatra, House of Dionysus, House of the Trident. Above the houses, the theater joins and sanctuaries for foreign gods like Isis and Serapis. A footpath with stairs leads up to the Kynthos, from where you have a panoramic view over the whole island.

Delos Transfers & Guided Tours

Only transfer (20 €)

	From Mykonos
Monday (01/04/-18/11)	10:00
	17:00
Tuesday-Sunday (01/04-18/11)	09:00
	10:00
	11:30
	15:00

Halfday-Trip to Delos, (01/04 - 18/11).

Fee: **50,00 €,** Children 6-12 J.: **25,00€.** under 6 years **free.**

The price includes: the boat trip, the entrance to the island and the guide.

Guided tours in the following language:

• English: Daily 10.00 + 17.00.

• For more information visit www.delostours.gr or info@delostours.gr

---

Accomodation/

Appartements

It's not surprising wisdom: Mykonos is expensive. But: if you know where, you can live cheap even in high season. Especially in early May, you can make real bargains.
Most travelers buy a guidebook after they have already booked the trip. So here are some tips for the *next* trip to Mykonos:

Apartments / Suites Sahas
Tel: +30 22890 22112
Mobile +30 693 6826864
info@sahas-mykonos.gr

Sahas

At the northern end of the city, just 500 meters from the Old Town and New Harbor, you will find Studios Sahas. Nocturnal tranquility, fabulous views of the Aegean Sea and the harbor, the rooms have a standard that beats - in relation to the price - other houses clearly. Extremely friendly and extremely clean, some rooms with jacuzzi.

Sahas

***

Aphrodite Beach Hotel
Kalafati Beach, Kalafati 846 00
Tel: +30 2289 071367
aphrodite-mykonos.com

Of course, it can also be a bit more luxurious. But then it should be right on the beach, as here right on Kalafati. 20 minutes from the center, but quiet.

****

Hotel Elysium
elysiumhotel.com
School of Fine Arts, Mykonos 846 00 Tel.: +30 2289 023952

Popular GLBT hotel with spacious rooms and a beautiful hillside location. The pool area with bar is a hot spot in the evening, as many guests from other hotels want to enjoy the sunset from there. Only 500 meters from the center, but: the steep road is a stress test for every bypass.

****

Hotel Eleni

Rohari Str., Mykonos 846 00 Tel: +30 2289 023457

www.elena mykonos.gr

For years popular hotel right in the center of the city, yet relatively quiet, as located in a side street.

Eleni

****

Hotel Semeli

Laka, Mykonos 84600

www.semelihotel-mykonos.com

If you love modern and elegant ambience, this is the place for you: friendly service, individual suites and a pool area with lots of plants.

Restaurants

On Mykonos you get everything, except a Big Mac. It gets harder if you want to go out for a decent price. The rule that a restaurant with many locals must be good, is definitely true on Mykonos. Be careful in restaurants on the beach. Therefore, it is worthwhile to have an early look at the map.

MYKONOS CITY

LOTUS in the Matogianni
Small restaurant with excellent international cuisine.

Nikos tavern behind the town hall
Based on the rush easy to find. Popular for decades, mainly because of the fish dishes

Eva's Garden
Kalogera 47
International cuisine in a nice ambience.

On the way from the parking lot to the old town you will pass the Salparo and the **Kavas** - the best fish restaurants of the city. Especially the Kavas is an institution.

Leto
On the waterfront, just before the harbor.
The oldest restaurant in the city in a beautiful garden. Chef is here the former personal chef of the Libyan dictator Gaddafi.

Burro
At the ring road between the two roundabouts.
Kitchen only until 17 o'clock, but very popular with late risers.

Kasarma

On the waterfront. Well attended all day. Known for its deep-fried sardines.

FAST AND CHEAP

Some may regret it, the others do not: McDonald's, KFC or subway: you won´t find them on Mykonos.

Air Fast Chicken

Towards Ano Mera, next to the proton supermarket.
No highlight in terms of ambience, but if you are really hungry and do not want to wait long, this is the place for you. Half the chicken for 6 euros is a bargain on Mykonos (and twice as big as a normal chicken).

Souvlaki Story

With three branches in the old town and now also on the road to Ano Mera left, successful and popular chain. Large portions at good prices.

Kalo Livadi

Solymar

Not cheap, but first-class service and high celebrity factor. International kitchen.

Agios Stefanos

Limnios

Greek cuisine at its best. Always well filled with locals - rightly so.

Ornos

Apaggio
Greek cuisine, wide selection of fish dishes.

Agios Sostis

Kikis - there are also Greeks in the queue. That says it all!

Cafés

Da Vinci

Directly on the promenade, just next to the town hall you will find the ice cream parlor "Da Vinci". Meeting point after dinner for Greeks and guests. Known for its sweets (crepes) and yogurt ice cream.

Calendar &Flight plans 2021

In the orthodox calendar, Easter and Pentecost 2021 are FOUR weeks later than ours (one week difference in normal years). The season therefore begins at the Greek Easter (Easter Sunday is May 2nd).
Most beaches are already prepared, and shops are open, but most clubs are not. They usually open on the 2nd weekend in May and close at the end of September.

Flights to Mykonos are already heavily booked, even in May and September. Please book quickly. Generally speaking, the best time to book flights to Mykonos is in October for the following summer. It is always a question of price. Return flights for May already cost 300 euros in some cases. Mykonos is no 29-euro destination - unfortunately or thank God. And never hope for a last-minute flight, because there are usually no last-minute flights to Mykonos.

Three tips:
If you don't mind changing flights, you can fly with Aegean from Düsseldorf/Munich via

Thessaloniki and Athens. Elaborate, but inexpensive.
Second option: fly from/via Vienna (with Ryanair/Wizz).
Or a cheap flight to Athens and from there with Volotea to Mykonos.
Currently flying: Eurowings, Condor, Air Baltic, Aegean, Tuifly, Ryanair and Wizz from Germany/Austria DIRECTLY to Mykonos (code JMK).

THE BEST OFFERS ARE WIZZ (from Vienna) and RYANAIR (from Frankfurt).

FROM COLOGNE: Eurowings
FROM DÜSSELDORF: Condor Wednesday (From 12.5. - 13.10.)
FROM FRANKFURT: Condor Wednesday (From 12.5. - 13.10.)
Ryanair Monday + Thursday (3. 6. - 30.9.)
FROM MUNICH:
Condor Saturday (01.05. - 16.10.)
Eurowings Friday + Sunday (08.05. - 17.10.)
FROM ZURICH: Edelweiss
FROM VIENNA: Ryanair and Wizz.

ATTENTION:
Sometimes the airlines cancel badly booked flights, especially in May and October.

Unfortunately, they are allowed to do so until 14 days before departure WITHOUT CLAIM OF DAMAGE. It is difficult to find replacement flights in May and October. The last resort is always Aegean via Athens or Thessaloniki.

If no direct flight can be found: Change in Munich (Condor/Eurowings), Vienna (RYANAIR/Wizz) or Athens (Aegean, Volotea, Sky Express, Olympic).

But be careful: the 20-minute flight from Athens to Mykonos is often more expensive than the flight from Germany to Athens!

Museums

Mykonos is certainly not a cultural destination with a large museum landscape. Who was on Delos, has actually fulfilled his stint. Nevertheless, it is worth visiting one or the other museum, so to speak en passant, when strolling through the old town. The "House of Lena" (Museum of Local History) is a small cute museum, which shows the way of life of the islanders and also brings back some old craftsmanship to life. Next to it is the Maritime

Museum, which is reminiscent of the former livelihood of the islanders. Valuable nautical charts are among the highlights of the collection. Both museums can be found at Three-Fountains-Square (see map p. 50).

At the Old Harbor East you will find the "Archaeological Museum".

It was built in the early 1900's to house the remains of the Rinia archaeological site. The building was of a neo-classical design in its original form but underwent a great deal of success

Repairs and additions of years 1935 and 1970 its Cycladic form with flat roofs. Admire the famous pottery, the imposing statues and the extraordinary pieces of jewelery.
The museum contains six rooms and exhibits collections of sculptures and sarcophagi by Rinia, as well as important finds from the excavations on Mykonos. The rich collection of pottery represents the Cycladic pottery. The pottery collection includes vases from artisan workshops in the Cyclades of the 9th and 8th centuries BC.
The most famous exhibit is the urn with reliefs from the case of Troy, seen in room E.

In room D, tombstones of Rinia are exhibited, on which stands the column of Tertias Orarias. In room A you will find pots of Mykonos, miniatures, jewelry and weapons. Tombstones, statues, inscriptions and a sarcophagus of Rinia were set up on the terrace.

The museum is open daily (except Mondays) from 8:30 to 15:00. Tel. 22890-22325.

Folk Museum Mykonos

In Kastro, the oldest district of the island's capital, Mykonos Town, which was named after the medieval castle, is the Folklore Museum of the island. The exhibition was housed in 1958 on the Venetian hill immediately behind the town hall in the residential building of a former sailor and captain, built in the 18th century.
Visitors to the museum can visit a wide variety of past everyday objects. For example, you can see a wide selection of old and new household appliances, old furniture and ceramics. Interested guests will also find an enormous collection of old scales and other measuring units, oil lamps, bowls, plates, locks

and keys. On the basis of a reconstructed kitchen and a bedroom, the sometimes quite difficult life and everyday situation in the time of the 19th century is brought to the visitors. In addition, small and large ship models as well as cannons from the war of independence carried out during the 19th century are shown.

Book recommendations
No publisher ad!

Non-fiction books about Mykonos are few, as the history of the island is of little interest.
But there are enough good thrillers and novels about Mykonos, of which I can recommend:
Most well-known are the thrillers of the series "Mikonos Crime" by Paul Katsitis. With 164 pages each for under 9 euros perfect for beach or plane. The main figure is Chief Commissioner Angelos Nikakis and - of course - he is gay and married. Sometimes a bit brutal, but entertaining.

The Problem: Until 2019 all books were only published in German and Greek.

BUT: Hooray, the first books IN ENGLISH have been published in 2020:

Mikonos Crime 1: Abducted
Mikonos Crime 2: Confusion
Mikonos Crime 3: The Prince
Mikonos Crime 4: The beast
Mikonos Crime 5: Spy

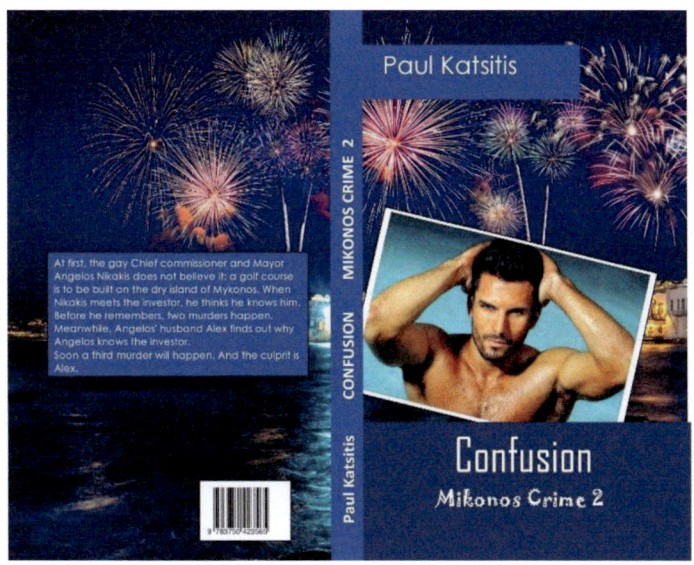

Published in GERMAN/GREEK:

Mykonos Crime 1 Die Bestie von Mykonos
Mykonos Crime 2 Rache
Mykonos Crime 4 Der Drei-Sterne-Mord
Mykonos Crime 5 Tattoo
Mykonos Crime 6 Skalpell
Mykonos Crime 7 Hass
Mykonos Crime 8 Sturm über Mykonos
Mykonos Crime 9 Die Maske
Mykonos Crime 10 Abseits
Mykonos Crime 11 Glut
Mykonos Crime 12 Putsch
Mykonos Crime 13 Royals
Mykonos Crime 14 Traumata
Mykonos Crime 15: Khaled
Mykonos Crime 17 Botschafter
Mykonos Crime 18 Libido
Mykonos Crime 19 Carneval

Mykonos Crime 20 Darknet
Mykonos Crime 21 Yariv
Mykonos Crime 22 Pontifex
Mykonos Crime 23 Sisa
Mykonos Crime 24 Kodex

Photo credit:

Backside: I-stockphoto,
Page 10, 64: sahas
Page 16: rene boulay
Page 34 wikimedia / olaf exchange
Page 37: andischatz
Page 44: wikipedia
Page 47: Julia Maudlin
Page 50: pexels
Page 59: wikipedia
Page 67: Mustang Joe.
Card: wikivoyage
City Map: ontheworldmap
All other recordings: Nikolaidis

A Kastro/Little Venice
B Parking
C Busterminal Port
D Promenade
E Busterm. Fabrika-Pl.
F Anlegest. SeaBus
Red Area: Main Shopping Area

Mykonos, Little Venice (shutterstock)

Old Mykonos around 1950

What is the island actually called?

Correct is "Mikonos" - pronounced "Meekonos".
But almost everyone spells it "Mykonos" and says
"Mükonos" (just like the German "ü" or the French
"u").
The inhabitants are called "Miconians".

Corona/Entry to Greece

Noone knows if the whole shit is over in summer
2021.
If not, there might be the same rules as in 2020.
You will need an online visa to enter the country.
Application under www.travel.gov.gr.
(For each family member individually!).

You will receive the visa **only 24 hours before**
departure in the form of a QR code, which you
can also print out. No entry without code!
If you do not receive a code, please print out the
confirmation mail. Some tourists have to make a
covid-test, depending on the QR-code and have
to stay the first night in the hotel.
If Corona is history, you only need your identity
card (EU-Citizens).

Rules

In 2020:
All restaurants/beach clubs had to close at midnight. Dancing was not allowed.
In shops you have to wear a mask, also in the old town.
The situation was critical in 2020. The quarantine hotel in Kalo Livadi was full von July to September.
Not surprising: a lot of young people and the crowd in the old town – perfect for the virus.

Check the rules before departure on the website of your foreign ministry.